A TASTE OF ENGLAND

THE ESSENCE OF ENGLISH COOKING, WITH 30 CLASSIC RECIPES
SHOWN IN 100 EVOCATIVE PHOTOGRAPHS

ANNETTE YATES

LORENZ BOOKS

This edition is published by Lorenz Books, an imprint of Anness Publishing Ltd, Hermes House, 88–89 Blackfriars Road, London SE1 8HA; tel. 020 7401 2077; fax 020 7633 9499

www.lorenzbooks.com; www.annesspublishing.com

If you like the images in this book and would like to investigate using them for publishing, promotions or advertising, please visit our website www.practicalpictures.com for more information.

UK agent: The Manning Partnership Ltd; tel. 01225 478444; fax 01225 478440; sales@manning-partnership.co.uk
UK distributor: Book Trade Services; tel. 0116 2759086; fax 0116 2759090; uksales@booktradeservices.com; exportsales@booktradeservices.com
North American agent/distributor: National Book Network; tel. 301 459 3366; fax 301 429 5746; www.nbnbooks.com
Australian agent/distributor: Pan Macmillan Australia; tel. 1300 135 113; fax 1300 135 103; customer.service@macmillan.com.au
New Zealand agent/distributor: David Bateman Ltd; tel. (09) 415 7664; fax (09) 415 8892

Publisher: Joanna Lorenz
Editorial Director: Helen Sudell
Editors: Joanne Rippin, Rosie Gordon
Designers: Nigel Partridge, Ian Sandom
Photographer: Craig Robertson
Food preparation and styling: Fergal Connelly, Helen Trent
Proofreading Manager: Lindsay Zamponi
Production Controller: Helen Wang

ETHICAL TRADING POLICY

Because of our ongoing ecological investment programme, you, as our customer, can have the pleasure and reassurance of knowing that a tree is being cultivated on your behalf to naturally replace the materials used to make the book you are holding. For further information about this scheme, go to www.annesspublishing.com/trees

Material in this book has been previously published in *England's Heritage: Food and Cooking*

PUBLISHER'S NOTE

Although the advice and information in this book are believed to be accurate and true at the time of going to press, neither the authors nor the publisher can accept any legal responsibility or liability for any errors or omissions that may be made nor for any inaccuracies nor for any harm or injury that comes about from following instructions or advice in this book.

NOTES

Bracketed terms are intended for American readers.
For all recipes, quantities are given in both metric and imperial measures and, where appropriate, in standard cups and spoons. Follow one set of measures, but not a mixture, because they are not interchangeable.
Standard spoon and cup measures are level.
1 tsp = 5ml, 1 tbsp = 15ml, 1 cup = 250ml/8fl oz
Australian standard tablespoons are 20ml.
Australian readers should use 3 tsp in place of 1 tbsp for measuring small quantities.
American pints are 16fl oz/2 cups. American readers should use 20fl oz/2.5 cups in place of 1 pint for liquids.
Electric oven temperatures in this book are for conventional ovens. When using a fan oven, the temperature will probably need to be reduced by about 10–20°C/20–40°F. Since ovens vary, you should check with your manufacturer's instruction book for guidance.
The nutritional analysis given for each recipe is calculated per portion (i.e. serving or item), unless otherwise stated. If the recipe gives a range, such as Serves 4–6, then the nutritional analysis will be for the smaller portion size, i.e. 6 servings. Measurements for sodium do not include salt added to taste.
Medium (US large) eggs are used unless otherwise stated.

contents

introduction

The food of England has a history that stretches back more than six thousand years, beginning with the herding and subsistence farming of the Celts. Since then the English diet has been influenced by invasion and immigration, a global empire, social development, trade, technology, politics and fashion. Today, English people are used to fresh produce year-round thanks to international trade, yet rely on home-grown, seasonal foods for the best flavour.

A temperate climate and a variety of landscapes have given each region of England its own specialities. The lush, sunny fields of Kent have traditionally yielded fine hops and apples for beer and cider making. In the West Country, plenty of rainfall and sunshine make for excellent pasture, and the dairies produce world-renowned cheeses, especially sharp, tangy Cheddar. In southern England, the long, scenic coastlines yield daily catches of shellfish and mackerel, haddock, turbot and sea bream, traditionally served battered or simply fried with butter and a squeeze of lemon.

The Midlands are best known for producing great pork, lamb and beef, and are famous for favourites such as Melton Mowbray pork pies. A Hereford steak with melting Shropshire blue cheese is another truly regional meal. Further north, in Lancashire, the Lake District and beyond, specialities include freshwater fish, lamb, various pies and, of course, roast beef with Yorkshire pudding. The north-east, meanwhile, has a reputation for game, along with fresh catches from the chilly North Sea. Sheep are the principal livestock of this cold and rugged area, and are used for excellent meat and cheese.

The whole country produces grains, vegetables and soft fruits in abundance, with plenty of variety throughout the year. England is also known for its love of puddings and cakes, jams, custards and all things sweet. Again, the regions jealously

Above: The landscape of England is home to an established farming tradition. Sheep thrive on the excellent pasture, providing succulent spring lamb to eat.

guard their favourite sweet recipes, from Eccles cakes and Cumberland rum nicky in the northern counties to Chelsea buns, lardy cakes and Devonshire cream teas in the south.

The displacement caused by the industrial revolution when people left their rural homes for factory towns, followed by the extremes of the Victorian era and two world wars, temporarily gave English cooking a poor name. However, today England is once more able to take pride in its reputation for excellent natural produce. This is as it should be – plenty of sun and rain and long

Above: The regions of England are known for their own specialities.

Below: The south-east coastline is still fished for classic seaside favourites such as whelks and cockles.

traditions of farming and fishing produce a superb harvest that is fresh, affordable and readily accessible to all. This, alongside the nation's renewed passion for fine ingredients and good cooking, means that England has become a true food-lover's paradise.

The centres for food excellence have gravitated to London and other major cities, where residents and visitors can taste the best of the home-reared meats, fish and vegetables that are used with such enthusiasm in urban eateries by the country's celebrated new generation of chefs.

Following this lead, home cooks are once again digging over their own vegetable and fruit plots and turning away from bland convenience foods back to traditional, flavoursome fare.

This beautiful book is an introduction to England's best-loved recipes, with a selection of dishes that are a joy to prepare and an even greater pleasure to eat. From creamy, luxurious Devon Crab Soup to Roast Rib of Beef, and Pan-fried Dover Sole to Summer Pudding, the recipes here use some of England's finest produce, as well as butter and cream from the country's renowned dairies.

Below: Kent's orchards are famous for their fine cider and eating apples.

breakfasts

In medieval days the people of England simply ate bread and drank ale before a day in the fields. Over the centuries breakfast (or breaking the overnight fast) changed and, by the late 19th century, it was a more elaborate affair, with the tables of the wealthy laden with food. Such ostentation ended with two world wars, and a more modest approach followed, although the English are still proud of their hearty breakfasts.

Left: Fresh eggs are a staple breakfast food in England, and are generally scrambled, fried, soft-boiled or poached.

full English breakfast

A cooked breakfast is a special treat, a reminder of the 19th century when the buffet tables of the rich groaned with food. As well as bacon, sausages and eggs cooked in a variety of ways, there might also have been fish, kedgeree, potatoes, kidneys, chops, steaks, sliced cold meats and devilled chicken or pheasant.

Serves 4

225–250g/8–9oz small potatoes
vegetable oil, for grilling (broiling)
    and frying
butter, for grilling and frying
4 large or 8 small good quality
    sausages
4 tomatoes
8 rashers (strips) of lean back or
    streaky (fatty) bacon, preferably
    dry-cured
4 small slices of bread,
    crusts removed
4 eggs

1 Thinly slice the potatoes. Heat 15ml/1 tbsp of the oil with a knob of butter in a large frying pan, add the potatoes and cook over a medium heat for 10–15 minutes, turning them occasionally until they are golden and cooked through. Remove with a slotted spoon and keep warm in a low oven.

2 Meanwhile, grill or fry the sausages in a little oil until golden brown and cooked through (test by inserting a skewer in the centre – the juices should run clear). Keep warm.

3 Halve the tomatoes and top each half with a tiny piece of butter, then grill until they are soft and bubbling. At the same time, grill the bacon or fry it in a little oil. Keep warm.

4 Fry the bread in a little oil and butter over a medium-high heat until crisp and golden brown. Remove with tongs and drain on crumpled kitchen paper.

5 Crack the eggs into the hot frying pan and cook over a medium heat. As soon as the eggs are ready, serve the breakfast on warm plates.

Per portion Energy 731kcal/3046kJ; Protein 32.7g; Carbohydrate 35.3g, of which sugars 7.6g; Fat 52.2g, of which saturates 16.5g; Cholesterol 288mg; Calcium 185mg; Fibre 3.1g; Sodium 2049mg

omelette Arnold Bennett

This creamy, smoked haddock soufflé omelette was created for the post-theatre suppers of the famous English novelist, who often stayed at the Savoy Hotel in London after World War I. It is now served all over the world as a breakfast or supper dish, and is superb with a simple salad of watercress and fresh tomatoes.

Serves 2

175g/6oz smoked haddock fillet, poached and drained
50g/2oz butter, diced
175ml/6fl oz/¾ cup whipping or double (heavy) cream
4 eggs, separated
40g/1½oz mature (sharp) Cheddar cheese, grated
ground black pepper
watercress, to garnish

Cook's tip

To reduce saltiness, rinse the haddock in fresh water before you gently poach it in milk.

1 Remove and discard the skin and any bones from the haddock fillet by carefully pressing down the length of each fillet with your fingertips.

2 Using forks and following the grain of the flesh, flake the fish into chunks.

3 Melt half the butter with 60ml/4 tbsp of the cream in a small non-stick pan. When the mixture is hot but not boiling, add the fish. Stir gently, taking care not to break up the chunks of fish. Bring slowly to the boil, stirring, then cover the pan, remove from the heat and set aside to cool for 20 minutes.

4 Preheat the grill (broiler) to high. Mix the egg yolks with 15ml/1 tbsp of the cream. Season with ground black pepper, then stir into the fish. In a separate bowl, mix the cheese and the remaining cream. Stiffly whisk the egg whites, then fold into the fish mixture.

5 Heat the remaining butter in an omelette pan until foaming. Add the fish mixture and cook until it is browned underneath. Pour the cheese mixture evenly over the top and grill (broil) until it is bubbling. Serve immediately.

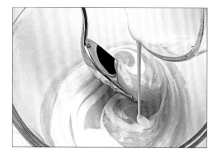

Per portion Energy 821kcal/3396kj; Protein 36.1g; Carbohydrate 2.6g, of which sugars 2.6g; Fat 74g, of which saturates 42.6g; Cholesterol 577mg; Calcium 280mg; Fibre 0g; Sodium 1123mg

Gateshead bacon floddies

This Tyneside breakfast is traditionally cooked in bacon fat and served alongside eggs and sausages. A kind of potato cake, floddies are said to have originated with canal workers, who cooked them on shovels over a fire. They should be served piping hot from the pan, as soon as they are crisp and golden brown.

1 Grate the potatoes on to a clean dish cloth, and squeeze and twist the towel to remove the liquid.

2 Mix the onion, potatoes, chopped bacon, flour and seasoning in a bowl, then add the eggs and blend well.

3 Heat the oil in a large frying pan. Add generous tablespoonfuls of the potato mixture to the hot oil and flatten them with a spatula.

4 Cook over a medium heat for 3–4 minutes on each side or until golden.

5 Drain the floddies on kitchen paper and serve at once.

Serves 4–6

250g/9oz potatoes, weighed
   after peeling
1 large onion, finely chopped
175g/6oz rindless streaky (fatty)
   bacon, finely chopped
50g/2oz/½ cup self-raising
   (self-rising) flour
2 eggs, beaten
vegetable oil, for frying
salt and ground black pepper

Per portion Energy 214kcal/891kJ; Protein 8.8g; Carbohydrate 17.1g, of which sugars 3.5g; Fat 12.7g, of which saturates 3.4g; Cholesterol 82mg; Calcium 38mg; Fibre 1.4g; Sodium 397mg

bubble and squeak

The name of this dish is derived from the noises the mixture makes as it cooks. Originally, it included chopped, boiled beef and was sprinkled with vinegar. This version is traditionally served with cold roast meat and pickles, but also goes very well with bacon and eggs for a filling and warming breakfast.

Serves 4

60ml/4 tbsp vegetable oil
1 onion, finely chopped
450g/1lb cooked, mashed
    potatoes
225g/8oz cooked cabbage,
    chopped
salt and ground black pepper

1 Fry the onion with 30ml/2 tbsp of the oil until soft but not browned.

2 Mix the potatoes and cabbage and season well with salt and pepper.

3 Stir the mix into the onions, then flatten it to form a cake. Fry over a medium heat for about 15 minutes, until browned underneath.

4 Invert the cake on to a large plate. Heat the remaining oil in the pan, then slip the cake back into the pan, browned side uppermost. Cook for about 10 minutes, until the underside is golden brown.

Per portion Energy 219kcal/908kJ; Protein 2.5g; Carbohydrate 17.2g, of which sugars 2.5g; Fat 15.9g, of which saturates 1.9g; Cholesterol 0mg; Calcium 33mg; Fibre 2.6g; Sodium 14mg.

kedgeree

Introduced from British-ruled India, kedgeree became popular in 18th-century England, when the original Hindi dish of rice, lentils and onion (*khitchri*) was adapted to English tastes by the addition of smoked fish and hard-boiled eggs. It is traditionally served for breakfast, but also makes a delicious lunch or supper dish.

Serves 4–6

450g/1lb smoked haddock
300ml/½ pint/1¼ cups milk
175g/6oz/scant 1 cup
    long grain rice
pinch each of grated nutmeg
    and cayenne pepper
50g/2oz butter
1 onion, finely chopped
2 hard-boiled eggs, shelled
salt and ground black pepper
lemon wedges and chopped fresh
    parsley, to garnish
buttered wholemeal (whole-wheat)
    toast, to serve

1 Gently poach the haddock in the milk, made up with just enough water to cover the fish, for about 8 minutes, or until just cooked. Lift out. Skin the haddock, remove all the bones and flake the fish with a fork. Set aside.

2 Bring 600ml/1 pint/2½ cups water to the boil in a large pan. Add the rice, cover closely with a lid and cook over a low heat for about 25 minutes, or until all the water has been absorbed by the rice. Season the cooked rice with salt and black pepper, nutmeg and cayenne pepper.

3 Meanwhile, heat 15g/½oz of the butter in a frying pan and fry the onion until soft and transparent. Set aside. Roughly chop one of the hard-boiled eggs and cut the other into neat wedges.

4 Stir the remaining butter into the hot rice and add the flaked haddock, onion and the chopped egg. Season to taste and heat the mixture through gently, stirring constantly. To serve, pile the kedgeree on to a warmed dish, sprinkle generously with parsley and arrange the wedges of egg on top. Garnish with lemon wedges and serve piping hot with buttered toast.

Per portion Energy 320kcal/1337kJ; Protein 15.6g; Carbohydrate 46.6g, of which sugars 0g; Fat 7.6g, of which saturates 3.2g; Cholesterol 149mg; Calcium 39mg; Fibre 0g; Sodium 357mg

soups and appetizers

Soups have always been a staple food in England – from simple, filling vegetable soups eaten by the poor, to the elegant broths with which the wealthy would begin a large, elaborate meal. Other savoury dishes whet the appetite with fine local ingredients such as early summer asparagus, smoked fish and superb dairy produce.

Left: Seasonal fruits and vegetables make an appearance in many appetizers, often married with local meat, fish and dairy produce.

Shropshire pea and mint soup

Peas have been grown in England since the Middle Ages, while mint was made popular by the Romans. Peas and mint picked fresh from the garden are still true summer treats and make a velvety, fresh-tasting soup. When fresh peas are out of season, or you are short of time, use frozen ones. Always use fresh mint.

Serves 6

25g/1oz/2 tbsp butter
1 onion, finely chopped
handful of fresh mint
675g/1½ lb shelled fresh peas
1.5ml/¼ tsp sugar
1.2 litres/2 pints/5 cups chicken
   or vegetable stock
150ml/¼ pint/⅔ cup double
   (heavy) cream
salt and ground black pepper
chopped fresh chives, to garnish

Cook's tip

A fresh, homemade vegetable stock with garden herbs lends the soup a wonderful flavour.

1 Melt the butter in a large pan and add the onion. Cook over a low heat for about 10 minutes, stirring occasionally, until soft and just beginning to brown.

2 Remove the stalks from the mint and chop or tear the leaves roughly.

3 Add the peas, sugar, chicken or vegetable stock and half the mint to the pan with the onions. Cover and simmer gently for 10–15 minutes until the peas are tender. If you are using frozen peas, reduce the cooking time to half.

4 Once the peas are cooked, remove from the heat and leave to stand for about 10 minutes, to allow the flavours to develop.

5 Add the remaining mint leaves to the peas. Stir, then pour all into a food processor and blend until smooth. If you do not have a food processor, press the mixture through a sieve (strainer). Return the soup to the pan.

6 Stir in the cream and reheat the soup gently without allowing it to boil. Season to taste and garnish with chopped chives.

Per portion Energy 121kcal/506kJ; Protein 6.1g; Carbohydrate 9.2g, of which sugars 5.2g; Fat 7g, of which saturates 4.2g; Cholesterol 18mg; Calcium 113mg; Fibre 3g; Sodium 123mg

Devon crab soup

Locals will tell you that crab caught around the Devon coastline is especially sweet. Although crab is available all the year round, it is at its best and is least expensive during the summer months – the perfect time to make this lovely creamy soup. Serve with farmhouse bread and fresh, unsalted dairy butter.

Serves 4–6

25g/1oz/2 tbsp butter
1 onion, finely chopped
1 celery stick, finely chopped
1 garlic clove, crushed
25ml/1½ tbsp plain (all-purpose)
    flour
225g/8oz cooked crab meat, half
    dark and half white
1.2 litres/2 pints/5 cups fish stock
30ml/2 tbsp dry sherry
150ml/¼ pint/⅔ cup double
    (heavy) cream
salt and ground black pepper

1 Melt the butter in a pan and add the onion, celery and garlic. Cook gently over a low to medium heat for about 5 minutes, stirring frequently, until the vegetables are soft but not browned.

2 Remove from the heat and quickly stir in the flour, then the brown crab meat. Gradually stir in the stock.

3 Bring the mixture just to the boil, then reduce the heat and simmer gently, half-covered, for about 30 minutes.

4 Pour the soup into a food processor and blend well. If you do not have a food processor or blender, then use a wooden spoon to press the soup through a sieve (strainer) twice. Clean the pan thoroughly. Return the soup to the clean pan. Season to taste with salt and pepper.

5 Chop the white crab meat and stir it into the pan with the sherry. Reheat the soup, stirring in the cream, but do not bring to the boil. Pour the soup into warmed bowls and serve it immediately with a grinding of black pepper.

  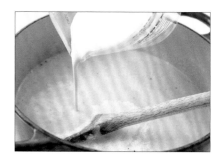

Per portion Energy 209kcal/867kJ; Protein 7.8g; Carbohydrate 4.6g, of which sugars 1.2g; Fat 17.3g, of which saturates 10.6g; Cholesterol 70mg; Calcium 69mg; Fibre 0.3g; Sodium 241mg

Sussex smokies

England's smokehouses produce some exceptional products. The flavour and colour of this Sussex dish is best when made with their pale, undyed smoked haddock rather than the bright yellow, artificially dyed variety. Follow this rich appetizer with a light, fresh main course for a beautiful summer lunch.

Serves 4

350g/12oz smoked haddock
450ml/¾ pint/scant 2 cups milk
25g/1oz/2 tbsp butter
25g/1oz/4 tbsp plain (all-purpose) flour
115g/4oz mature (sharp) Cheddar cheese, grated
60ml/4 tbsp fresh breadcrumbs
salt and ground black pepper
crusty bread, to serve

Cook's tip

Halve the amount of haddock and use lightly smoked salmon fillets with shelled prawns for a luxurious, pink and white version of the dish.

1 Remove and discard all skin and bones from the smoked haddock and cut the fish into strips. Set aside.

2 Put the milk, butter, flour and seasoning into a pan. Remember that the cheese and haddock are salty, so do not add too much salt at this stage. Over a medium heat and whisking constantly, bring to the boil and bubble gently for 2–3 minutes until you have a thick, smooth sauce. Do not overcook the sauce or stop stirring, as this may cause it to burn on to the bottom of the pan and spoil the flavour of the sauce.

3 Add the haddock pieces and half the grated cheese to the hot sauce and heat it nearly to boiling point, so that the cheese melts. Stir the mixture gently with a wooden spoon, keeping the fish pieces intact.

4 Divide the mixture between individual flameproof dishes or ramekins. Toss together the remaining cheese and the breadcrumbs and sprinkle the mixture over the top of each filled dish. Put the dishes under a hot grill (broiler) until bubbling and golden. Serve immediately with crusty bread.

Per portion Energy 363kcal/1525kJ; Protein 30.1g; Carbohydrate 21.8g, of which sugars 5.8g; Fat 17.4g, of which saturates 10.8g; Cholesterol 79mg; Calcium 396mg; Fibre 0.5g; Sodium 1073mg

pears with Stilton cream and walnuts

English cheeses and fruit taste wonderful together, and traditional combination include apple pie with Wensleydale or Cheshire cheese with fruit cake. This dish needs pears that are ripe, yet firm – Comice, Conference or Williams all work well.

Serves 6

115g/4oz/½ cup cream cheese or curd cheese
75g/3oz Stilton cheese
30ml/2 tbsp single (light) cream
115g/4oz/1 cup roughly chopped walnuts
6 ripe pears
15ml/1 tbsp lemon juice
salt and ground black pepper

mixed salad leaves and 6 cherry tomatoes, to serve
walnut halves and sprigs of fresh flat leaf parsley, to garnish

For the dressing
juice of 1 lemon
a little finely grated lemon rind
pinch of caster (superfine) sugar
60ml/4 tbsp olive oil

1 Mash the cream cheese and Stilton together with plenty of black pepper, then beat in the cream. Stir in 25g/1oz/¼ cup of the chopped walnuts. Cover the mixture and chill.

2 Peel the pears with a vegetable peeler and halve them lengthways. Scoop out the cores. Submerge the pears in a bowl of cold water with the lemon juice to prevent them from browning.

3 Whisk the dressing ingredients together and season to taste.

4 Divide the salad leaves and tomatoes between the plates and sprinkle the remaining walnuts over.

5 Drain the pears well, then turn them in the dressing and arrange on the salad.

6 Pile the cheese into the cavities of the pears and spoon over the rest of the lemon dressing. Garnish with walnut halves and parsley.

Per portion Energy 407kcal/1684kJ; Protein 7.1g; Carbohydrate 16.7g, of which sugars 16.6g; Fat 34.9g, of which saturates 11.3g; Cholesterol 33mg; Calcium 100mg; Fibre 4.1g; Sodium 164mg

potted cheese

The potting of cheese became popular in the 18th century, and it is still a great way to use up odd pieces left on the cheeseboard. Blend them with your chosen seasonings, adjusting the flavour before adding the alcohol.

Serves 4–6

250g/9oz hard cheese, such as
   Cheddar, roughly chopped
75g/3oz/6 tbsp soft unsalted
   butter, plus 50g/2oz for melting
1.5ml/¼ tsp ready-made English
   (hot) mustard
1.5ml/¼ tsp ground mace
30ml/2 tbsp sherry
ground black pepper
fresh parsley, to garnish

1 Put the cheese into the bowl of a food processor. Use the pulse button to chop it into small crumbs.

2 Add the butter, mustard, mace and a little black pepper and blend again until smooth. Taste and adjust the seasoning. Finally, blend in the sherry.

3 Spoon the mixture into a dish just large enough to leave about 1cm/½in to spare on top. Level the surface.

4 Melt 50g/2oz butter in a small pan, skimming off any foam. Leaving the

sediment in the pan, pour a layer of melted butter on top of the cheese mixture to cover the surface. Chill.

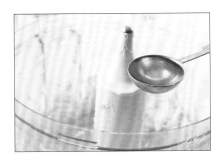

5 When ready to serve, garnish with parsley and serve spread generously on hot toast or crispbreads.

Per portion Energy 262kcal/1082kJ; Protein 10.7g; Carbohydrate 0.2g, of which sugars 0.2g; Fat 23.6g, of which saturates 15.2g; Cholesterol 70mg; Calcium 290mg; Fibre 0g; Sodium 363mg

asparagus with hollandaise sauce

Since the 16th century, England has produced this 'queen of vegetables', at its finest for a short season in early summer. Serve it simply – drizzled with melted butter, with lightly boiled eggs (dip the asparagus into the egg) or, as here, with hollandaise sauce – a luxurious appetizer or accompaniment to poached salmon.

Serves 4

2 bunches of asparagus
30ml/2 tbsp white wine vinegar
2 egg yolks
115g/4oz butter, melted
juice of ½ lemon
salt and ground black pepper

Cook's tips

• Asparagus is also good served cold with mayonnaise.
• Make stock with the woody ends of the asparagus rather than throwing them away and add them to vegetable soups or sauces.

1 Snap the tough ends off the asparagus spears and discard. Tie into four bundles. Bring a pan of water to the boil while you prepare the sauce.

2 In a small pan, bring the vinegar to the boil and bubble until it has reduced to just 15ml/1 tbsp. Remove from the heat and add 15ml/1 tbsp cold water. Whisk the egg yolks into the vinegar and water mixture, then put the pan over a very low heat and continue whisking until the mixture is frothy and thickened. You could use a bain-marie or double boiler for this stage, but if using a regular pan keep the heat low and whisk carefully.

3 Remove from the heat again and slowly whisk in the melted butter. When the sauce is nearly ready, drop the asparagus spears into the fast boiling water, cooking for 1–2 minutes until just tender. Test the thickest part of the stalk with a small sharp knife for tenderness; take care not to overcook. Meanwhile, add the lemon juice to the sauce and season to taste.

4 Pile the drained asparagus on to warmed plates and spoon over the hollandaise sauce. Season lightly if you wish and serve the dish at once.

Per portion Energy 276kcal/1135kJ; Protein 5.3g; Carbohydrate 2.7g, of which sugars 2.6g; Fat 27.1g, of which saturates 15.9g; Cholesterol 162mg; Calcium 51mg; Fibre 2.1g; Sodium 180mg

main courses

In England, meat or poultry feature in most meals, and are served in many different ways, from casseroles and grills to curries. Famously, the country takes great pride in its Sunday roast – a succulent joint of prime meat cooked to perfection in the oven and served with all the trimmings. There is also a great tradition of fishing around the extensive coastline, and dishes such as fish and chips and scallops with bacon are perennial favourites.

Left: England has fine natural resources, with good pasture and abundant shoreline and rivers, allowing cooks a huge choice of local produce.

pan-fried Dover sole

For many, Dover sole is one of the finest of the flat fish, often called 'the Englishman's fish of choice' because in the days when transport was slow its flavour actually improved during the journey from the Kent coast. Use herbs such as dill, parsley or tarragon. Extra lemon wedges on the side are essential.

Serves 4

4 small Dover sole, dark skin and
   fins removed
30–45ml/2–3 tbsp flour seasoned
   with salt and ground black
   pepper
45ml/3 tbsp olive oil
25g/1oz/2 tbsp butter
juice of 1 lemon
15ml/1 tbsp chopped fresh herbs
lemon wedges and watercress
   sprigs, to garnish

1 Spread the seasoned flour on a plate, and coat each fish, carefully shaking off any excess so that each fillet is lightly covered.

2 Heat a large non-stick frying pan and add the oil. Add one or two fish to the pan and cook over a medium heat for 3–5 minutes on each side until golden brown and cooked through. Lift them out and keep them warm while you cook the remaining fish.

3 Add the remaining oil and the butter to the hot pan and heat until the butter has melted. Stir in the lemon juice and chopped herbs. Drizzle the pan juices over the fish and serve immediately, garnished with lemon wedges and watercress sprigs.

Cook's tips

• Leaving the white skin on one side of the fish helps to keep its shape during cooking; it is also full of flavour and good to eat, particularly the crisp edges.
• To grill (broil) the fish, omit the flour and brush both sides with melted butter. Cook under a medium grill (broiler) for 5–7 minutes on each side until golden.

Per portion Energy 177kcal/739kJ; Protein 18.6g; Carbohydrate 3g, of which sugars 0.2g; Fat 10.2g, of which saturates 1.2g; Cholesterol 50mg; Calcium 42mg; Fibre 0.3g; Sodium 101mg

fish and chips

Here is one of England's most recognized dishes. Use white fish of your choice – cod, haddock, hake, huss, plaice, skate or whiting – and cook in batches so that each piece of fish and all the chips are perfectly crunchy.

Serves 4

115g/4oz/1 cup self-raising (self-rising) flour
150ml/¼ pint/⅔ cup water
675g/1½lb potatoes
oil, for deep-frying
675g/1½lb skinned cod fillet
salt and ground black pepper

1 Stir the flour and salt together in a bowl, then make a well in the centre. Gradually whisk in the water to make a smooth batter. Leave to stand for 30 minutes.

2 Using a sharp knife, cut the potatoes into strips about 1cm/½in wide and 5cm/2in long. Put the potatoes in a colander and rinse them with cold water, then drain and dry well.

3 Heat the oil in a deep-fryer or large heavy pan to 150°C/300°F. Using a wire basket, lower the potatoes in batches into the hot oil and cook for 5–6 minutes, shaking the basket occasionally until the chips (French fries) are soft but not browned. Remove the half-cooked chips from the oil and drain them thoroughly on crumpled kitchen paper.

4 Increase the heat of the oil to 190°C/375°F. Cut the fish into four pieces and season with salt and pepper. Stir the batter, then dip the fish into it, one piece at a time, allowing the excess to drain off.

5 Working in two batches if necessary, lower the fish into the hot oil and fry for 6–8 minutes, until crisp and brown. Drain the fish on kitchen paper and keep warm in a medium oven (not too hot, as the fish is kept steamy-hot in its batter casing).

6 Make sure the oil is hot again then add a batch of half-cooked chips, cooking for 2–3 minutes, until brown and crisp. Keep hot while cooking the other batches. Sprinkle the chips with salt and serve with the fish on warmed plates. Mushy peas and lemon wedges make ideal accompaniments.

Per portion Energy 521kcal/2188kJ; Protein 36.3g; Carbohydrate 48.9g, of which sugars 2.6g; Fat 21.3g, of which saturates 2.7g; Cholesterol 78mg; Calcium 126mg; Fibre 2.6g; Sodium 223mg

scallops with bacon

In the 19th century, scallops were dredged in large numbers along the Sussex coast. Today, they are fished off the Isle of Man. Like oysters, scallops are thought a luxury, and often believed to be an aphrodisiac. They are best when cooked briefly, and the smoky flavour of bacon with scallop is a heavenly combination.

Serves 2

15ml/1 tbsp olive oil

4 streaky bacon (fatty) rashers (strips), cut into 2.5cm/1in pieces

2–3 fresh sage leaves, chopped

small piece of butter

8 large or 16 small scallops

15ml/1 tbsp fresh lemon juice

100ml/3¾fl oz dry (hard) cider or dry white wine

1 Heat the oil in a frying pan. Add the bacon and sage and cook, stirring occasionally, until the bacon is golden brown. Lift out and keep warm.

2 Add the butter to the pan and when hot add the scallops. Cook quickly for about 1 minute on each side until browned. Lift out and keep warm.

3 Add the lemon juice and cider or wine to the pan and, scraping up any sediment remaining in the pan, bring just to the boil. Continue bubbling gently until the mixture has reduced to just a few tablespoons of syrupy sauce.

4 Serve the scallops and bacon with the sauce drizzled over.

Cook's tip

In summer, some fishmongers sell marsh samphire (glasswort), which grows around the coast of England and makes a good accompaniment to this dish. To prepare samphire, wash it well and pick off the soft fleshy branches, discarding the thicker woody stalks. Drop it into boiling water for just 1 minute before draining and serving on warmed plates.

Per portion Energy 416kcal/1734kJ; Protein 31.2g; Carbohydrate 4.8g, of which sugars 1.4g; Fat 29g, of which saturates 11.8g; Cholesterol 106mg; Calcium 38mg; Fibre 0g; Sodium 890mg

traditional roast chicken

Try to use a free range, organic chicken for this recipe – it has the best taste. Traditional accompaniments are sausages and roast potatoes, added alongside the chicken part way through roasting. Par-boil the potatoes first for the best results.

Serves 6

1 chicken weighing about
   1.8kg/4lb, with giblets and neck
1 small onion, sliced
1 small carrot, sliced
small bunch of parsley and thyme
15g/½oz/1 tbsp butter
30ml/2 tbsp vegetable oil
6 rashers (strips) streaky (fatty)
   bacon
15ml/1 tbsp plain
   (all-purpose) flour
salt and ground black pepper

For the stuffing

1 onion, finely chopped
50g/2oz/4 tbsp butter
150g/5oz/2½ cups fresh white
   breadcrumbs
15ml/1 tbsp chopped fresh
   parsley
15ml/1 tbsp chopped mixed fresh
   herbs, such as thyme, marjoram
   and chives
grated rind and juice of ½ lemon

1 Put the giblets and neck into a pan with the sliced onion, the carrot and the bunch of parsley and thyme. Season with salt and pepper. Cover generously with cold water, bring to the boil and simmer for about 1 hour. Strain the stock and set aside, discarding the giblets. Preheat the oven to 200°C/400°F/Gas 6.

2 To make the stuffing, cook the onion in the butter in a large pan over a low heat until soft and just turning golden. Remove from the heat and stir in the breadcrumbs, herbs, lemon rind and juice, and salt and pepper.

3 Spoon the stuffing into the neck cavity of the chicken and secure the opening with a small skewer. Weigh the stuffed chicken and calculate the cooking time at 20 minutes per 450g/1lb plus 20 minutes extra. Spread butter over the chicken breast, then put the oil into a roasting pan and sit the bird in it. Season and lay the bacon rashers over the breast to keep it moist.

4 Put the chicken into the hot oven. After 20 minutes, reduce the temperature to 180°C/350°F/Gas 4 and cook for the remaining time. To check the chicken is cooked, insert a sharp knife between the body and the thigh: if the juices run clear with no hint of blood, it is done.

5 Transfer the chicken to a serving dish and allow it to rest for 10 minutes before carving. Meanwhile make the gravy. Pour off the excess fat from the roasting pan and sprinkle in the flour. Cook gently, stirring, for 1–2 minutes. Gradually stir in 300ml/½ pint/1¼ cups of the reserved stock.

6 Bring to the boil, stirring and adding extra stock if necessary. If you have steamed or boiled vegetables to go with the meal, add the cooking water to the gravy if it is too thick. Adjust the seasoning and serve with the meal.

Per portion Energy 823kcal/3420kJ; Protein 55.7g; Carbohydrate 21.1g, of which sugars 19.1g; Fat 57.8g, of which saturates 19.7g; Cholesterol 383mg; Calcium 113mg; Fibre 4.9g; Sodium 252mg

coronation chicken

Originally devised as part of the feast to celebrate the coronation of Elizabeth II in 1953, this creamy, curry-flavoured chicken salad has been a favourite on celebration buffet tables, as well as a filling for sandwiches, ever since.

Serves 8

½ lemon
1 chicken, about 2.25kg/5lb
1 onion, quartered
1 carrot, quartered
large bouquet garni
8 black peppercorns, crushed
salt and ground black pepper
watercress sprigs, to garnish
lettuce and crusty bread, to serve

For the sauce

1 small onion, chopped
15g/½oz/1 tbsp butter
15ml/1 tbsp curry paste
15ml/1 tbsp tomato purée (paste)
125ml/4fl oz/½ cup red wine
1 bay leaf
juice of ½ lemon, or to taste
10ml/2 tsp apricot jam
300ml/½ pint/1¼ cups mayonnaise
125ml/4fl oz/½ cup whipping
cream

1 Put the lemon half in the chicken cavity, then place it in a close-fitting pan. Add the vegetables, bouquet garni, peppercorns and a little salt.

2 Add water to come two-thirds of the way up the chicken. Bring to the boil. Cover and cook gently for 1½ hours, until the chicken juices run clear. Leave to cool then remove the skin and bones and chop the flesh.

3 To make the sauce, cook the onion in the butter until soft. Add the curry paste, tomato purée, wine, bay leaf and lemon juice, then cook gently for 10 minutes. Add the jam, press through a sieve (strainer) and cool the sauce completely.

4 Beat the cooled curry sauce into the mayonnaise. Whip the cream and fold it in; add seasoning and lemon juice, then stir in the chicken pieces.

5 Serve the chicken on a bed of crisp lettuce leaves, garnished with watercress sprigs, with crusty bread.

Per portion Energy 587kcal/2429kJ; Protein 10.1g; Carbohydrate 17.1g, of which sugars 4.7g; Fat 51.6g, of which saturates 8.8g; Cholesterol 228mg; Calcium 97mg; Fibre 1.1g; Sodium 401mg

toad in the hole

Early versions of toad in the hole, in the 18th century, were made with pieces of meat, such as sirloin steak or lamb chops. Today the 'toads' are sausages and the crisp batter is the same as that used for Yorkshire pudding.

Serves 6

175g/6oz/1½ cups plain
   (all-purpose) flour
2.5ml/½ tsp salt
2 eggs
300ml/½ pint/1¼ cups milk
30ml/2 tbsp vegetable oil
500g/1¼lb sausages

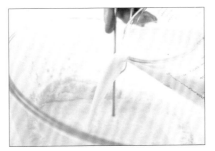

1 Preheat the oven to 220°C/425°F/ Gas 7. For the batter, sift the flour and salt into a bowl, make a well in the centre and break the eggs into it. Add the milk mixed with 300ml/½ pint/1¼ cups cold water. Gradually mix the flour and liquid, whisking to a smooth batter. Leave to stand.

2 Pour the oil into a roasting pan and add the sausages. Bake for about 10 minutes until the oil is very hot and the sausages begin to brown.

3 Stir the batter and quickly pour it around the sausages and return to the oven. Cook for about 45 minutes or until the batter is set and golden.

Per portion Energy 497kcal/2070kJ; Protein 14.5g; Carbohydrate 32.1g, of which sugars 3.8g; Fat 35.4g, of which saturates 13.6g; Cholesterol 109mg; Calcium 141mg; Fibre 1.3g; Sodium 616mg

steak and kidney pudding

This classic dish is in fact a 19th-century invention that has, in a relatively short time, become one of England's most famous specialities. In Victorian days it would have included oysters, and some versions today contain mushrooms.

Serves 6

500g/1½lb lean stewing steak, cut into cubes
225g/8oz beef kidney or lamb's kidneys, skin and core removed and cut into small cubes
1 onion, finely chopped
30ml/2 tbsp finely chopped fresh herbs, such as parsley and thyme
30ml/2 tbsp plain (all-purpose) flour
275g/10oz/2½ cups self-raising (self-rising) flour
150g/5oz/1 cup shredded suet (US chilled, grated shortening)
finely grated rind of 1 small lemon
about 120ml/4fl oz/½ cup beef stock or water
salt and ground black pepper

Cook's tips
• Replace the kidneys with whole or halved button (white mushrooms) if you prefer.
• Use stout or brown ale and beef stock to make a rich gravy.

1 Put the stewing steak into a large mixing bowl and add the kidneys, onion and chopped herbs. Mix in the plain flour and seasoning.

2 To make the pastry, sift the self-raising flour into another large bowl. Stir in the suet and lemon rind. Add cold water to bind the ingredients and gather into a soft dough.

3 On a lightly floured surface knead the dough gently, and then roll out to make a circle about 35cm/14in across. Cut out one-quarter of the circle, roll up and put aside.

4 Lightly butter a 1.75 litre/3 pint heatproof bowl. Line the bowl with the dough, allowing the pastry to overlap the top of the bowl.

5 Spoon the steak mixture into the bowl, packing it in carefully. Pour in sufficient stock or water to reach three-quarters of the way up the filling.

6 Roll out the reserved pastry into a circle and lay it over the filling. Pinch the edges together to seal them well.

7 Cover with greaseproof (waxed) paper or baking parchment, pleated in the centre to allow the pudding to rise, then with a sheet of foil (again pleated at the centre).Tuck the edges under and press them tightly to the sides of the bowl until sealed (or tie with string). Steam for about 5 hours.

8 Remove the foil and paper, slide a knife around the sides of the pudding and turn out on to a warmed plate. Serve it with mashed potato, green vegetables and extra gravy to pour over.

Per portion Energy 436kcal/1835kJ; Protein 31.1g; Carbohydrate 49.5g, of which sugars 4.8g; Fat 13.9g, of which saturates 3.6g; Cholesterol 166mg; Calcium 201mg; Fibre 1.9g; Sodium 380mg

rib of beef with Yorkshire puddings

Yorkshire puddings, originally a separate first course, have been eaten with roast beef since the 18th century. Roast potatoes are also essential accompaniments, par-boiled and added to the roasting pan part way through cooking.

Serves 6–8

rib of beef joint, about 3kg/6½lb
vegetable oil, for brushing
salt and ground black pepper

For the Yorkshire puddings
115g/4oz/1 cup plain (all-purpose)
   flour
1.5ml/¼ tsp salt
1 egg
200ml/7fl oz/scant 1 cup milk
vegetable oil or beef dripping, for
   greasing

For the horseradish cream
60–75ml/4–5 tbsp finely grated
   fresh horseradish
300ml/½ pint/1¼ cups sour cream
30ml/2 tbsp cider vinegar or white
   wine vinegar
10ml/2 tsp caster (superfine)
   sugar

For the gravy
600ml/1 pint/2½ cups beef stock

1 Preheat the oven to 220°C/425°F/Gas 7. Weigh the joint and calculate the cooking time required as follows: 10–15 minutes per 500g/1¼lb for rare beef, 15–20 minutes for medium and 20–25 minutes for well done.

2 Put the joint into a large roasting pan. Brush it all over with oil and season with salt and pepper. Put into the hot oven and cook for 30 minutes, until the beef is browned. Lower the oven temperature to 160°C/325°F/Gas 3 and cook for the calculated time, spooning the juices over the meat occasionally.

3 For the Yorkshire puddings, sift the flour and salt into a bowl and break the egg into it. Make the milk up to 300ml/½ pint/1¼ cups with water and gradually whisk into the flour to make a smooth batter. Leave to stand while the beef cooks. Generously grease eight Yorkshire pudding tins (muffin pans) measuring about 10cm/4in.

4 For the horseradish cream, put all the ingredients into a bowl and mix well. Cover and chill until required.

5 At the end of its cooking time, remove the beef from the oven, cover with foil and leave to stand for 30–40 minutes before carving and serving.

6 Meanwhile, increase the oven temperature to 220°C/425°F/Gas 7 and put the prepared tins on the top shelf for 5 minutes until very hot. Pour in the batter and cook for about 15 minutes until well risen, crisp and golden brown.

7 To make the gravy, transfer the beef to a warmed serving plate. Pour off the fat from the roasting pan, leaving the meat juices. Add the stock to the pan, bring to the boil and bubble until reduced by about half. Season to taste.

Per portion Energy 1037kcal/4338kJ; Protein 129g; Carbohydrate 15.1g, of which sugars 4.1g; Fat 51.5g, of which saturates 24.3g; Cholesterol 352mg; Calcium 123mg; Fibre 0.5g; Sodium 249mg

Lancashire hotpot

This famous hotpot was traditionally cooked in a farmhouse or communal bread oven, in time for supper at the end of the day. The ingredients would have been layered straight into the pot, but here the meat is first browned to add colour and extra flavour to the dish. Use tender spring lamb for a melt-in-the-mouth dish.

Serves 4

15ml/1 tbsp vegetable oil
8–12 lean best end of neck (cross rib) lamb chops
175g/6oz lamb's kidneys, skin and core removed and cut into pieces
2 onions, thinly sliced
a few sprigs of fresh thyme or rosemary
900g/2lb potatoes, thinly sliced
600ml/1 pint/2½ cups lamb or vegetable stock
25g/1oz/2 tbsp butter, cut into small pieces
salt and ground black pepper

1 Preheat the oven to 180°C/350°F/Gas 4. Heat the oil in a large frying pan, then brown the lamb chops quickly on all sides. Remove the meat from the pan and set aside.

2 Add the kidneys to the hot pan and brown lightly over a high heat. Lift out.

3 In a casserole, layer the chops and kidneys with the onions, herbs and potatoes, seasoning each layer with salt and pepper.

4 Finish off with a layer of potatoes. Pour over the stock, sprinkle with herbs and dot the top with butter. Cover and cook in the oven for 2 hours.

5 Remove the lid, increase the oven temperature to 220°C/425°F/Gas 7 and cook, uncovered, for a further 30 minutes until the potatoes are crisp.

Variation

Add sliced carrots or mushrooms to the layers. Replace 150ml/¼ pint/⅔ cup of the stock with dry (hard) cider or wine.

Per portion Energy 810kcal/3400kJ; Protein 76.7g; Carbohydrate 43.7g, of which sugars 9.3g; Fat 37.8g, of which saturates 13.2g; Cholesterol 363mg; Calcium 140mg; Fibre 6.2g; Sodium 285mg

sweet treats

The English are famous for their sweet
tooth and for the fruity, creamy or rich
puddings that have traditionally featured at
the end of lunch and dinner, as well as the
cakes or scones enjoyed at teatime.
Seasonal fruits are often a main ingredient,
raw, stewed or baked, and made into
all sorts of delicious concoctions.
The desserts and puddings featured here
are just a tantalizing taster of the array that
English cuisine has to offer.

*Left: Strawberries are the classic English soft
fruit, and enjoyed from June to August with
cream or in various fabulous desserts.*

lemon meringue pie

This popular dessert is a 20th-century development of older English cheesecakes – open tarts with a filling of curds. It was relished in the 1950s after the years of wartime rationing, when sugar, lemons and eggs became plentiful once more.

Serves 6

115g/4oz/1 cup plain
   (all-purpose) flour
pinch of salt
50g/2oz/4 tbsp butter, diced
50g/2oz/¼ cup cornflour
   (cornstarch)
175g/6oz/¾ cup caster
   (superfine) sugar
grated rind and juice of 2 lemons
2 egg yolks
15g/½oz/1 tbsp butter, diced

For the meringue topping

2 egg whites
75g/3oz/½ cup caster (superfine)
   sugar

1 Rub the butter into the salted flour until the mixture resembles breadcrumbs. Stir in about 20ml/4 tsp cold water until you can make a ball of dough. Wrap the pastry and chill for 30 minutes. Preheat the oven to 200°C/400°F/Gas 6.

2 Roll out the pastry and line a 20cm/8in flan tin (pan). Prick the base with a fork, line with baking parchment and add baking beans. Bake the pastry case (pie shell) for 15 minutes. Remove the beans and parchment and cook for 5 more minutes. Remove, and reduce the temperature to 150°C/300°F/Gas 2.

3 To make the filling, put the cornflour into a pan and add the sugar, lemon rind and 300ml/½ pint/1¼ cups water. Bring to the boil, stirring as it thickens. Reduce the heat and simmer gently for 1 minute. Remove the pan from the heat and stir in the lemon juice. Add the egg yolks one at a time, beating after each addition, then stir in the butter. Pour the mixture into the pastry case.

4 To make the meringue, whisk the egg whites until stiff peaks form, then whisk in half the sugar. Fold in the rest of the sugar using a metal spoon. Heap the meringue over the lemon filling, covering it completely. Cook for about 20 minutes until lightly browned.

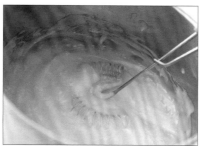

Per portion Energy 357kcal/1497kJ; Protein 6.8g; Carbohydrate 42.8g, of which sugars 25.1g; Fat 18.9g, of which saturates 9g; Cholesterol 129mg; Calcium 108mg; Fibre 0.7g; Sodium 137mg

Bakewell tart

This is a modern version of the Bakewell pudding, which is made with puff pastry and has a custard-like almond filling. It is said to be the result of a 19th-century kitchen accident and is still baked in the original shop in Bakewell, Derbyshire. This very simple, tart-like version is a tea-time treat.

Serves 4

For the pastry
115g/4oz/1 cup plain
  (all-purpose) flour
pinch of salt
50g/2oz/4 tbsp butter, diced

For the filling
30ml/2 tbsp raspberry jam
2 whole eggs and 2 extra yolks
115g/4oz/generous ½ cup caster
  (superfine) sugar
115g/4oz/½ cup butter, melted
55g/2oz/⅔ cup ground almonds
a few drops of almond extract
icing (confectioners') sugar,
  to dust

1 Sift the flour and salt and rub in the butter until it resembles fine crumbs.

2 Stir in about 20ml/4 tsp cold water and gather into a smooth ball of dough. Wrap in clear film (plastic wrap) and chill for 30 minutes. Preheat the oven to 200°C/400°F/ Gas 6.

3 Roll out the pastry and use to line an 18cm/7in loose-based flan tin (pan). Spread the jam over the pastry.

4 Whisk the eggs, egg yolks and sugar together in a large bowl until the mixture is thick and pale.

5 Gently stir in the melted butter, ground almonds and almond extract.

6 Pour the mixture over the jam in the pastry case (pie shell). Put the tart into the hot oven and cook for 30 minutes until just set and browned. Sift a little icing sugar over the top before serving warm or cold.

Per portion Energy 700kcal/2919kJ; Protein 10.8g; Carbohydrate 57.1g, of which sugars 36.7g; Fat 49.9g, of which saturates 17.1g; Cholesterol 257mg; Calcium 110mg; Fibre 0.9g; Sodium 394mg

queen of puddings

This delicate dessert has a base made with custard and breadcrumbs flavoured with lemon. Once it is set, a layer of jam is added and covered with a light meringue topping. Mrs Beeton called this Queen of Bread Pudding. It's good served just as it is, or with cream or condensed milk.

Serves 4–6

80g/3oz/1½ cups fresh
    breadcrumbs
60ml/4 tbsp caster (superfine)
    sugar, plus 5ml/1 tsp
grated rind of 1 lemon
600ml/1 pint/2½ cups milk
4 eggs
45ml/3 tbsp raspberry jam,
    warmed

1 Stir the breadcrumbs, 30ml/2 tbsp of the sugar and the lemon rind together in a bowl. Bring the milk to the boil in a pan, then stir it into the breadcrumb and sugar mixture.

2 Separate three eggs and beat the yolks with the whole egg. Stir into the breadcrumb mixture, then pour into a buttered ovenproof dish and leave to stand for 30 minutes.

3 Meanwhile, preheat the oven to 160°C/325°F/Gas 3. Cook the pudding for 50–60 minutes, until set.

4 Whisk the egg whites in a clean bowl until stiff, then gradually whisk in the remaining 30ml/2 tbsp caster sugar until the mixture is thick.

5 Spread the jam over the custard, then spoon the meringue over.

6 Ensure the meringue covers the top in peaks, which will brown and crisp. Sprinkle the remaining 5ml/1 tsp sugar over the meringue, then return the pudding to the oven for a further 15 minutes, until the meringue is light golden. Serve warm.

Per portion Energy 297kcal/1259kJ; Protein 13.7g; Carbohydrate 45g, of which sugars 31g; Fat 8.5g, of which saturates 3.2g; Cholesterol 199mg; Calcium 242mg; Fibre 0.4g; Sodium 281mg

jam roly poly

This warming winter pudding, with its childish name, first appeared on English tables in the 1800s. A savoury version known as plough pudding was eaten by Victorian stable lads on chilly days. While boiling is the traditional cooking method for roly poly, baking produces a lovely golden crust.

Serves 4–6

175g/6oz/1½ cups self-raising
   (self-rising) flour
pinch of salt
75g/3oz shredded suet
   (US chilled, grated shortening)
finely grated rind of 1 small lemon
90ml/6 tbsp jam

1 Preheat the oven to 180°C/350°F/Gas 4. Line a baking sheet with baking parchment.

2 Sift the flour and salt into a bowl and stir in the suet and lemon rind. Stir in cold water, a little at a time, with a metal spatula until you can gather the mixture into a soft ball with your fingers. On a lightly floured work surface or board, knead the dough very lightly with floured hands until it is smooth and pliable.

3 Gently roll out the pastry into a rectangle that measures approximately 30 x 20cm/12 x 8in. Using the metal spatula, spread the jam evenly over the pastry, leaving the side edges and ends clear.

4 Brush the edges of the pastry with a little water and, starting at one of the short ends, carefully roll up the pastry. Be careful not to squeeze out the jam.

5 Place the roll, seam side down, on the prepared baking sheet. Cook for 30–40 minutes until risen, golden and cooked through. Leave the pudding to cool for a few minutes before cutting into thick slices to serve.

To boil the roly poly
1 Shape the mixture into a roll and wrap loosely (to allow room for the pudding to rise) in baking parchment and then in a large sheet of foil. Twist the ends of the paper and foil to seal them securely and tie a string handle from one end to the other.

2 Lower the package into a pan of boiling water, cover and boil for about 1½ hours. Check the water occasionally and top up with boiling water if necessary.

Per portion Energy 240kcal/1008kJ; Protein 2.8g; Carbohydrate 33.7g, of which sugars 10.7g; Fat 11.3g, of which saturates 5.7g; Cholesterol 0mg; Calcium 104mg; Fibre 0.9g; Sodium 111mg

apple and blackberry crumble

The origins of crumble are unclear. It did not appear in recipe books until the 20th century, but has become a firm favourite all over the country. Autumn heralds the harvest of apples and their perfect partners, soft, sweet blackberries. The oatmeal is a great addition to the traditional crumble topping, giving it a pleasant crispness.

Serves 6–8

115g/4oz/½ cup butter
115g/4oz/1 cup wholemeal
  (whole-wheat) flour
50g/2oz/½ cup fine oatmeal
50g/2oz/¼ cup soft light brown
  sugar
a little grated lemon rind
  (optional)
900g/2lb cooking apples
450g/1lb/4 cups blackberries
squeeze of lemon juice
175g/6oz/scant 1 cup caster
  (superfine) sugar

1 Preheat the oven to 200°C/400°F/Gas 6. To make the crumble, rub the butter into the flour, and then add the oatmeal and brown sugar and continue to rub in until the mixture begins to stick together to form large crumbs.

2 Mix in the grated lemon rind if using. Peel and core the cooking apples and slice into wedges.

3 Put the fruit, lemon juice, 30ml/2 tbsp water and the caster sugar in a shallow ovenproof dish, about 2 litres/3½ pints/9 cups capacity.

4 Cover the fruit evenly with the crumble topping. Put the crumble into the hot oven and cook for 15 minutes, then reduce the heat to 190°C/375°F/Gas 5 and cook for a further 15–20 minutes until golden brown, with bubbling juices at the edges.

5 Let the crumble rest for about 10 minutes before serving, as the fruit filling will be extremely hot. Serve hot with clotted cream, vanilla ice cream or fresh custard. Leftovers may be reheated or eaten cold.

Per portion Energy 336kcal/1413kJ; Protein 4g; Carbohydrate 53.1g, of which sugars 30.8g; Fat 13.4g, of which saturates 6.8g; Cholesterol 27mg; Calcium 72mg; Fibre 3g; Sodium 81mg

bread and butter pudding

Plates of white bread and butter were for many years a standard feature of an English tea or nursery supper, and frugal cooks needed to come up with ways to use up the leftovers. Bread and butter pudding was a favourite homemade pudding but often finds its way on to restaurant menus today.

Serves 4–6

50g/2oz/4 tbsp soft butter
about 6 large slices of day-old
   white bread
50g/2oz dried fruit, such as
   raisins, sultanas (golden raisins)

or chopped dried apricots
40g/1½oz/3 tbsp caster
   (superfine) sugar
2 large (US extra large) eggs
600ml/1 pint/2½ cups full cream
   (whole) milk

1 Preheat the oven to 160°C/325°F/ Gas 5. Lightly butter a 1.2 litre/2 pint/5 cup ovenproof dish.

2 Butter the bread and cut into small triangles or squares. Arrange half the pieces, buttered side up, in the dish and sprinkle the dried fruit and half of the sugar over the top.

3 Lay the rest of the bread slices buttered side up on top of the fruit. Sprinkle over the remaining sugar.

4 Beat the eggs lightly together, just to mix the yolks and whites, and stir in the milk. Strain the egg mixture and pour it over the bread in the dish. Push the top slices down into the liquid with a spatula if necessary, to ensure that the custard is evenly absorbed. Leave the pudding to stand for 30 minutes.

5 Bake for about 45 minutes or until the custard is set and the top is crisp and golden brown.

Per portion Energy 622kcal/2597kJ; Protein 10.5g; Carbohydrate 55.6g, of which sugars 37.8g; Fat 39g, of which saturates 23g; Cholesterol 186mg; Calcium 203mg; Fibre 1.6g; Sodium 350mg

Eton mess

This pudding gets its name from the famous public school, Eton College, where it is served at the annual picnic on 4 June. The "mess" consists of whipped cream, crushed meringue and sliced or mashed strawberries. It looks and tastes wonderful, and there's no better way to eat the summer's finest strawberries.

Serves 4

450g/1lb ripe strawberries
45ml/3 tbsp elderflower cordial or
    orange liqueur
300ml/½ pint/1¼ cups double
    (heavy) cream
4 meringues or meringue baskets

1 Hull the strawberries and slice into a bowl, reserving a few for a garnish.

2 Sprinkle with the elderflower cordial or fruit liqueur. Cover the bowl and chill for about 2 hours.

3 Whip the cream until soft peaks form. Crush the meringue into small pieces. Add the fruit and most of the meringue to the cream and fold in lightly with a metal spoon.

4 Spoon into serving dishes and chill. Do not make too far in advance, as the meringue will soften. Before serving, decorate with the reserved strawberries and meringue.

Per portion Energy 526kcal/2182kJ; Protein 3.5g; Carbohydrate 32.8g, of which sugars 32.8g; Fat 40.4g, of which saturates 25.1g; Cholesterol 103mg; Calcium 60mg; Fibre 1.4g; Sodium 53mg

fruit trifle

Everyone's favourite, trifle is a classic English dessert. The earliest trifles were simple blends of custard and fruit purée, but this recipe, which harks back to the 18th century, is the fruit, sponge and custard layered dish we know and love today.

Serves 6–8

450ml/¾ pint/scant 2 cups full
   cream (whole) milk
1 vanilla pod (bean)
3 eggs
25g/1oz/2 tbsp caster (superfine)
   sugar
1 x 15–18cm/6–7in plain sponge
   cake
225g/8oz/¾ cup raspberry jam
150ml/¼ pint/⅔ cup medium or
   sweet sherry
450g/1lb ripe fruit, such as pears
   and bananas, peeled and sliced
300ml/½ pint/1¼ cups whipping
   cream
toasted flaked (sliced) almonds, to
   decorate

1 To make the custard, heat the milk in a pan with the vanilla pod, split along its length, and bring almost to the boil. Remove from the heat. Leave to cool a little while you whisk the eggs and sugar together lightly. Remove the vanilla pod and gradually whisk the milk into the egg mixture.

2 Rinse out the pan with cold water and return the mixture to it. Stir over a low heat until the custard thickens enough to coat the back of a wooden spoon; do not let it boil. Pour the custard into a jug (pitcher), cover and set aside.

3 Halve the sponge cake horizontally, spread with the raspberry jam and sandwich together. Cut into slices and use to line the bottom and lower sides of a large glass serving bowl.

4 Sprinkle the sponge cake with the sherry. Spread the fruit over the sponge in an even layer. Pour the custard on top, cover with clear film (plastic wrap) to prevent a skin forming, and leave to cool and set. Chill until required.

5 To serve, whip the cream and spread it over the custard. Decorate with the almonds. Serve immediately, or keep for up to 12 hours in the refrigerator.

Per portion Energy 631kcal/2615kJ; Protein 8.4g; Carbohydrate 24.9g, of which sugars 18.4g; Fat 53.1g, of which saturates 28.4g; Cholesterol 258mg; Calcium 155mg; Fibre 1.4g; Sodium 116mg

summer pudding

This stunning dessert is an essential part of the English summer and it is deceptively simple to make. Use a mixture of seasonal soft fruits and a good quality loaf of white bread. Serve the pudding cold with lashings of thick cream or yogurt. For an extra fruity kick, pour over raspberry coulis.

Serves 4–6

about 8 x 1cm/½in-thick slices
   of day-old white bread,
   with crusts removed
800g/1¾lb/7 cups mixed berries,
   such as strawberries,
   raspberries, blackcurrants,
   redcurrants and blueberries
50g/2oz/¼ cup golden caster
   (superfine) sugar
lightly whipped double (heavy)
   cream or thick yogurt, to serve

Variation

Make a delicious autumn pudding by using stewed apples and blackberries instead of the soft summer fruits.

1 Trim a slice of bread to fit the base of a 1.2 litre/2 pint/5 cup bowl, then trim another 5–6 slices to line the sides, ensuring the bread stands above the rim.

2 Place all the fruit in a pan with the sugar. Do not add any water. Cook very gently for 4–5 minutes until the juices begin to run. The fruit should retain some shape and texture. Allow it to cool.

3 Spoon the fruit, with enough of the juices to soak into the bread, into the bread-lined bowl. Any remaining juice can be served with the pudding.

4 Fold over the excess bread, then cover the fruit with the remaining slices, trimming to fit. Place a small plate or saucer that fits inside the bowl directly on top of the pudding. Weight it down with a 900g/2lb weight, if you have one, or use a couple of full food cans.

5 Chill the pudding in the refrigerator for at least 8 hours or overnight. To serve, run a knife between the pudding and the bowl and turn out on to a plate. Spoon any reserved juices over the top, and serve with cream or yogurt.

Per portion Energy 192kcal/815kJ; Protein 5.2g; Carbohydrate 43.1g, of which sugars 22.1g; Fat 1g, of which saturates 0g; Cholesterol 0mg; Calcium 82mg; Fibre 2.5g; Sodium 245mg

scones with jam and cream

For most people, English afternoon tea without a plate of scones would be unthinkable. They are equally good served with cream and soft fruit, such as strawberries or raspberries. It's important that they are freshly baked, but they are quick and easy to make, and the baking smell is wonderful.

Makes about 12

450g/1lb/4 cups self-raising (self-rising) flour, or 450g/1lb/ 4 cups plain (all-purpose) flour and 10ml/2 tsp baking powder
5ml/1 tsp salt
55g/2oz/¼ cup butter, chilled and cut into small cubes
15ml/1 tbsp lemon juice
about 400ml/14fl oz/1⅔ cups milk, plus extra to glaze
jam and whipped double (heavy) cream, to serve

1 Preheat the oven to 230°C/450°F/Gas 8. Sift the flour, baking powder (if using) and salt into a mixing bowl, and stir to mix through. Add the butter and rub it into the flour until the mixture resembles fine breadcrumbs.

2 Whisk the lemon juice into the milk and leave for about 1 minute to thicken slightly, then pour into the flour mixture and mix quickly to make a soft but pliable dough. The softer the mixture, the lighter the scones will be, but if it is too sticky they will spread and lose their shape while baking. Knead the dough briefly, then roll it out on a lightly floured surface to at least 2.5cm/1in thick.

3 Using a 5cm/2in biscuit (cookie) cutter, and dipping it into flour each time, stamp out rounds. Place the dough rounds on a well-floured baking sheet. Re-roll the trimmings and cut out more scones.

4 Brush the tops of the scones with milk, then bake for about 20 minutes, or until risen and golden brown. Remove from the oven and wrap the scones in a clean dish towel to keep them warm and soft until ready to eat. Eat the scones with plenty of jam and a generous dollop of clotted or whipped double cream.

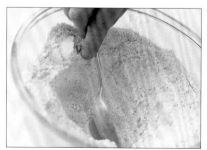

Per scone Energy 177kcal/749kJ; Protein 4.7g; Carbohydrate 30.7g, of which sugars 2.2g; Fat 4.8g, of which saturates 2.8g; Cholesterol 12mg; Calcium 93mg; Fibre 1.2g; Sodium 43mg

index

kedgeree 14